Sir Francis Drake

Jason Hook

Illustrations by Clyde Pearson

Great Lives

Beethoven
Louis Braille
Captain Cook
Marie Curie
Sir Francis Drake
Einstein
Queen Elizabeth I
Queen Elizabeth II
Anne Frank
Gandhi
King Henry VIII
Helen Keller

John F. Kennedy
Martin Luther King
John Lennon
Ferdinand Magellan
Karl Marx
Mary Queen of Scots
Napoleon
Florence Nightingale
Elvis Presley
William Shakespeare
Tchaikovsky
Mother Teresa

P060310987

Editor: Penny McDowell

First published in 1988 by
Wayland (Publishers) Limited
61 Western Road, Hove
East Sussex BN3 1JD, England

© Copyright 1988 Wayland (Publishers) Ltd

British Library Cataloguing in Publication Data
Hook, Jason
    Sir Francis Drake. – (Great lives).
    1. Drake, *Sir* Francis, *1540?–1596*
    Juvenile literature
    I. Title   II. Series
    942.05′5′0924   DA86.22.D7

    ISBN 1–85210–176–8

Phototypeset by Kalligraphics Ltd, Redhill, Surrey
Printed and bound in Italy by G. Canale C.S.p.A., Turin

Contents

The game of bowls   4

A sailor's apprenticeship   6

Spanish treachery   8

The treasure house of the world   10

The Queen's pirate   12

Mutiny and Magellan's Strait   14

'The Dragon'   16

The longest voyage   18

Sir Francis Drake   20

Singeing the King's beard   22

The mighty Armada   24

Devil ships   26

The beating of the drum   28

Important dates   30

Books to read   30

Glossary   31

Index   32

The game of bowls

The ocean groaned under their weight, as 125 ships of the mighty Spanish Armada gathered in the English Channel. Merchantmen laden with provisions clustered together with nimble scout ships in a crescent-moon formation several kilometres wide. Galley slaves hauled great square-sailed **galleasses**, their hulls large enough to house chapels. At the crescent's horns, majestic, heavily-armed galleons with one metre thick stern timbers built up into towering, gilded 'castles', plunged and rolled on the waves.

Pennants and flags fluttered above painted sails decorated with the fleet's scarlet cross; castles, dragons and wolves identified the parts of Spain which the ships came from. Trumpets sounded and drums rumbled above the moan of taut rigging and the whinnying of cavalry horses. The Armada seemed invincible.

King Philip II of Spain, a devout Catholic who accused England's Queen Elizabeth I of **heresy** because of her Protestant beliefs, had declared the Armada's voyage to be a holy

crusade. The Armada was part of a plan to overthrow Queen Elizabeth I and so create a Catholic monarchy. The flagship *San Martin* flew a vast, silk banner depicting Jesus and the Virgin Mary, and carried with it the Pope's blessing.

On 29 July 1588 Captain Thomas Fleming breathlessly delivered news of the Armada's approach to Lord Admiral Howard, who was, according to legend, playing bowls on Plymouth Hoe with his Vice-Admiral, Sir Francis Drake. Drake was renowned as the

When news of the Spanish Armada's approach arrived, Lord Admiral Howard and Vice-Admiral Sir Francis Drake were playing bowls on Plymouth Hoe.

'Queen's pirate' for having led many daring raids against the Spanish. Knighted as the first Englishman to sail around the world, he was the popular hero of his country.

With typical calmness, Drake is said to have declared to his fellow players: 'We have time enough to finish the game and beat the Spaniards, too.'

A sailor's apprenticeship

Francis Drake was born about 1541, in his grandparents' farmhouse in Tavistock, Devon, the first of Edmund Drake's twelve sons. While at sea, Edmund had been converted to the new Protestant faith spreading through Europe. The Protestants were passionately opposed by the Roman Catholics who strictly followed the rulings of the Pope.

In 1549, King Edward VI's introduction of a new church prayer book caused Catholic peasants to riot in Cornwall and Devon. The Drake family fled for their lives.

They found a new home in Kent, living in the leaky hull of an abandoned ship, moored on the River Medway near Chatham dockyard. Edmund Drake became a 'reader of prayers' to the king's soldiers, preaching the Protestant word.

At the age of about twelve, Francis went to sea as **apprentice** to the ageing captain of a time-worn ship. The tiny vessel guided great merchant ships into the English Channel,

Above *Edward VI, who introduced a new prayer book in 1549.*

6

ferried goods along the English coast, and occasionally pitched across the open sea to collect wine, hops and silks from Dutch and French ports.

Voyages across treacherous tidal waters gave Francis experience of the sea which could never be mastered by reading books. He was so successful at sea that when his old master died he bequeathed his ship to Francis in his will. Drake, not yet twenty, was now equipped to pursue the **mariner's** profession in which his fame would be unequalled.

Rioting in Cornwall and Devon caused the Drake family to flee their farmhouse in Tavistock and move into the leaky hull of a ship on the River Medway.

Spanish treachery

Indian slaves on a Spanish sugar plantation in the West Indies.

In 1493, Pope Alexander VI divided up the **New World** between Portugal and Spain. Spain jealously guarded her new wealth in the Americas, and all foreign ships sailing in the 'Spanish Main' around the Caribbean Sea were reported as pirates.

In 1562, Drake's cousin John Hawkins was engaged in the illegal and barbaric trading of African slaves to Spanish colonies in South America and the West Indies. Attracted by the promise of this **pioneering voyage**, Drake, in his early twenties, sold his ship and joined Hawkins in Plymouth.

Drake first crossed the Atlantic in 1566. The expedition's slave shipment was abandoned at Rio de la Hacha, when Spanish officials refused to trade.

Six weeks after returning to England, the ambitious Drake sailed again, on an expedition led by Hawkins himself. During the voyage he was made captain of the *Judith*. Upon reaching the Caribbean, Drake sailed ahead to Rio de la Hacha, where he opened

Left *Pirates attack a Spanish galleon hoping to find treasure.*

negotiations by sending two cannonballs through the Spanish Treasurer's house!

After suffering storm damage, the fleet anchored in San Juan de Ulua, off the coast of Mexico. Two days later the Spanish treasure fleet arrived with Don Martin, Viceroy of Mexico, aboard. After exchanging hostages to ensure peaceful conduct, Hawkins permitted the fleet to enter the harbour.

The following morning, the Spanish attacked. After ferocious fighting, the English survivors fled with Drake in the *Judith* and Hawkins in the *Minion*.

Drake vowed to avenge the Spanish betrayal, and later said of Don Martin: 'I would rather meet with him than with all the gold and silver in the Indies, that I might show him how to keep the word of a gentleman.'

The treasure house of the world

Drake married Mary Newman in Devon in July 1569. The following year, he captained a Caribbean trading expedition to recover the losses of his previous ill-fated voyage. The San Juan de Ulua treachery had convinced Drake that only piracy could capture Spanish gold.

So, in 1571, Drake sailed the tiny *Swan* to the Caribbean, to spy out the Panama Isthmus. Mule trains lumbered over this neck of land hauling Peruvian gold and silver from treasure ships anchored at Panama, on the Pacific coast, to the Caribbean port of Nombre de Dios. Befriending escaped slaves called 'Cimaroons', and discovering a lush, hidden bay called Port Pheasant, Drake plotted his assault on the Spanish Main.

In May 1572, Drake led seventy-three men in the *Swan* and *Pasco* across the Atlantic to his Port Pheasant lair. Concealing their ships, Drake's

From a high tree on the Panama Isthmus, Drake sighted the Pacific Ocean for the first time.

men sailed three smaller boats into Nombre de Dios. As the moon rose the Englishmen attacked in two groups. Sounding trumpets, beating drums and brandishing flaming **pikes**, Drake's followers forced the Spanish to flee.

Drake led his men to the Treasury, declaring: 'I have brought you to the treasure house of the world!' Then, suddenly, Drake collapsed, blood pouring from a bullet wound in his leg. His men retreated, carrying their leader to safety.

In May 1572, as night fell, Drake and his men attacked the port of Nombre de Dios saying that it was 'the treasure house of the world'.

Several months later, Drake's Cimaroon allies led him to a high ridge on the Panama Isthmus. Climbing a great tree, Drake glimpsed for the first time the Pacific Ocean. Filled with wonder, he prayed that 'Almighty God in his goodness would give me life and leave to sail once in an English ship upon that sea.'

11

The Queen's pirate

Drake sailed home from his voyage in a captured Spanish warship. He had abandoned the leaking *Pasco* and secretly ordered his ship's carpenter to **scuttle** the *Swan* when fever left him with too few men to sail her.

Drake had at last captured Spanish treasure after joining French **privateer** Guillaume Le Testu in an ambush north of Nombre de Dios. Hearing the jingling bells of a mule train laden with treasure from Panama, they had pounced upon the silver and gold that now filled the hold of Drake's ship.

Drake reached Plymouth on 9 August 1573. His new-found fame coincided with a reconciliation between Spain and England. Fearing Queen Elizabeth I's displeasure towards his exploits in the Spanish Main, Drake went to ground for two years.

In 1575, he served under Walter, Earl of Essex, against Catholic **mercenaries** stirring up rebellion in Ireland. Through his patron, and his secretary Thomas Doughty, Drake gained influence with important men in

Left *Drake fighting against the Spanish as the 'queen's pirate'.*

Queen Elizabeth I secretly supported Drake and his piracy.

court and government.

When relations between Spain and England soured once more, Drake received an audience with his Queen. She agreed secretly to support Drake's piracy against the Catholic might of Spain, so that King Philip's treasure might find its way into the Tower of London. To avoid war with the Spanish, she would assure them that Drake was a 'freebooter', an independent adventurer. Drake, though, now considered himself the Queen's 'privateer'.

Financed by Elizabeth I and her most prominent noblemen, Drake plotted a voyage into the waters he had gazed upon from the Cimaroon's look-out post – the Pacific Ocean.

Mutiny and Magellan's Strait

On 13 December 1577, the *Elizabeth, Marigold, Swan, Christopher* and Drake's stout flagship, the 100-tonne *Pelican*, set sail from Plymouth. Most of the 164 men aboard believed their destination to be Alexandria, Egypt.

After transferring the *Christopher*'s name and crew to a captured Portuguese **caravel**, the fleet reached the Cape Verde Islands. Here they claimed a Portuguese merchant ship, the *Mary*, whose wise, old sea pilot, Nuno da Silva, was taken aboard by Drake, to navigate the voyage.

Beyond the eerie **Doldrums** south of the Equator, Drake abandoned the *Swan, Christopher* and *Mary* in storms off the South American coast. His remaining vessels anchored in June 1578, off Port St Julian, where the **gibbet** still stood upon which Magellan had executed **mutineers** during his voyage around the world in 1520.

Drake also faced rebellion, led by Thomas Doughty, and gathering a jury of forty men, Drake convicted his friend of **mutiny** and witchcraft. After sharing communion and a banquet with his captain, Doughty was beheaded.

The route taken by Magellan on his epic voyage (1519–1521)

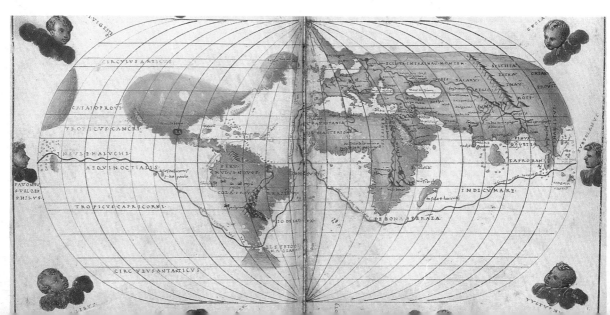

Brandishing the severed head, Drake proclaimed: 'This is the end of traitors!'

Sailing into Magellan's Strait with the fleet's morale restored, Drake rechristened the *Pelican Golden Hind*, after the crest of his patron Sir Christopher Hatton. Drake navigated the Strait in sixteen days – twenty-one fewer than Magellan.

Emerging in the Pacific on 6 September 1578, Drake was carried south by a terrifying storm. By chance he discovered that America could be rounded below Magellan's Strait.

The storm's fury wrecked the *Marigold* and sent the *Elizabeth* back to England. Drake sailed on in the *Golden Hind*.

Facing rebellion from some of his men, Drake beheaded the leader, Thomas Doughty.

'The Dragon'

Wounded by hostile Indians at Mocha Island, Drake pressed north to Valparaiso on Chile's coast, where the Spanish *Grand Captain of the South* was anchored. Since no English privateers ever prowled the Pacific, she assumed the *Golden Hind* to be friendly. Her welcoming drum roll signalled the start of Drake's raids on the Spanish Pacific coast, as his men swarmed aboard the ship, and plundered 25,000 pesos.

Sailing up the coast to North America, Drake rifled 360 kilograms of silver from a Spaniard's laden llama train.

At Callaos, Peru, Drake learnt of a magnificent treasure ship, *Cacafuego*, bound for Panama,

The Golden Hind *raiding the Spanish treasure ship* Cacafuego.

and unfurled all sail in pursuit. Drake spotted the ship on 1 March 1579, and in the evening he pounced, shooting away the *Cacafuego*'s **mizzen-mast** and claiming her dazzling cargo – chests of jewels, twenty-six tonnes of silver, thirteen trunks of silver coins, and thirty-six kilograms of gold.

The *Golden Hind* rode ever lower in the water, with her treasures of gold and silver, as Drake plundered Spanish nobleman Don Francisco de

In California, Drake won favour with the native Amerindians.

Zarate's galleon *Espirito Santo*, and raided Guatulco in Guatemala. In her wake, the Spaniards spread the terrifying news of the devilish English pirate 'El Draque' – 'The Dragon'.

Meanwhile Drake scoured the North American coast for the legendary 'North-West Passage', believed to lead to the Atlantic. Finding no such channel, he sheltered in June in a Californian bay, to repair his leaking ship. Here, Amerindians crowned Drake with a head-dress of feathers, and he claimed the land for Queen Elizabeth I, naming it Nova Albion.

The longest voyage

Drake sailed west in July 1579, into the seemingly endless Pacific. After two months he reached the Caroline Islands.

Further west, a heavy scent filled the air around the fabled Spice Islands, the Moluccas. Drake was greeted by the Sultan of Ternate, who had rebelled against his Portuguese rulers. The sultan agreed to trade with England, and the *Golden Hind* was loaded with six tonnes of precious cloves.

While navigating the scattered islands of Indonesia, the *Golden Hind*, with a fearful grating sound, suddenly struck a submerged reef. The crew worked desperately through the night of 9 January 1580 to save her. Eight cannon and half her spices were hurled overboard, and as the wind dropped the ship, miraculously intact, slid free.

From Java, Drake sailed for 118 days, across the Indian Ocean and around the Cape of Good Hope. Landing at Sierra Leone, the crew feasted greedily after the longest unbroken voyage ever.

On 26 September 1580, the *Golden Hind* and her fifty-nine surviving crew sailed into Plymouth. Francis Drake was the first Englishman to sail around the world.

On 13 December 1577, Sir Francis Drake set off in the Golden Hind *on his longest voyage, returning to Plymouth three years later.*

Sir Francis Drake

As news of the famous voyage spread across the country, Drake became 'all England's hero'. Adored by the common people and celebrated in ballads sold on street corners, he enjoyed the attentions of all the courts of Europe.

With the Spanish ambassador Mendoza furiously demanding the return of his country's treasures plundered by 'this vile **corsair**', Drake was summoned before Queen Elizabeth I.

As 'all England's hero', Drake was adored by his country.

Presenting her with the choicest jewels, he narrated his incredible exploits. Elizabeth ordered her share of the treasure to be carried to the Tower of London.

Amid lavish celebrations, the Queen visited the *Golden Hind* at Deptford on 4 April 1581. As Drake knelt before her, she whispered: 'Master Drake, the King of Spain has asked for your head, and we have a weapon here with which to remove it.' The gilded sword was laid upon Drake's shoulder as Queen Elizabeth proclaimed him a knight. Mendoza considered this a gross insult to his country, and in the following years Spain and England drifted rapidly towards open war.

The *Golden Hind* was preserved at Deptford, and Drake was elected Mayor of Plymouth, where he erected a compass 'to guide mariners to the fabled west.' After the death of his first wife, Drake married Elizabeth Sydenham, and they lived at the Buckland Abbey estate that Drake had bought with his treasures. Over the fireplace of his magnificent home hung Drake's coat of arms, with the motto: *Sic Parvis Magna* – 'Greatness from Small Beginnings.'

Queen Elizabeth I is welcomed on board the Golden Hind.

Singeing the King's beard

In 1585, King Philip II of Spain ordered the arrest of all English merchant vessels in his ports. In response, twenty-nine warships left Plymouth on 14 September, led by Sir Francis Drake's 600-tonne *Elizabeth Bonaventure*. They sailed first to Vigo Bay in Spain to proclaim 'The Dragon mightily at sea again.'

Sailing to the Caribbean, Drake conquered Santa Domingo, in **Hispaniola**, and Cartagena, capital of the Spanish Main, before fever forced the fleet homewards. After sacking the Spanish settlement of St Augustine, Florida, Drake carried home English settlers from Roanoke, Virginia, in the New World, reaching Plymouth on 28 July 1586.

The voyage demoralized the Spaniards, and Philip II found Europe's banking houses reluctant to finance his armies.

When Spain's **shipwrights** began building an Armada to invade England, Drake sailed once more. With customary boldness, he led twenty-six ships against the busy Spanish port of

Cadiz on 19 April 1587. The English ships' cannons destroyed over thirty Spanish vessels, and with black smoke swirling overhead, Drake darted into the inner harbour to plunder the Marquis of Santa Cruz's galleon.

Next Drake stormed Sagres Castle, and established a base at Cape St Vincent. All ships sailing past here to join the Armada were seized.

Seeking greater treasures, Drake ventured to the Azores, where on 8 June he captured the enormous Portuguese ship, *San Felipe*, owned by King Philip II. Overflowing with gold, china, spices, jewels and silks, she was

Francis Drake's arch enemy King Philip II of Spain .

the richest prize ever taken. Drake sailed triumphantly into Plymouth on 26 June 1587, declaring, 'I have singed the King of Spain's beard.'

As the English attack, Spanish ships burn in Cadiz harbour.

The mighty Armada

Drake's treasure haul, and his destruction of the Armada's ships and stores, forced Spain's sailors to stay in harbour for a year.

In May 1588, England's Lord Admiral, Howard of Effingham, sailed to Plymouth to assume command of his fleet. Raising his vice-admiral's flag, Drake accepted the position of second-in-command with good grace.

While Queen Elizabeth I negotiated in the vain hope of peace, Drake begged her permission to attack Spain's ports once more. She eventually agreed, but Drake's daring July expedition to intercept the Armada was driven back to Plymouth by cruel winds. Here the fleet idled when, on 29 July, Drake's game of bowls was interrupted by news of the Armada's arrival.

That night, the fleet sailed from Plymouth, as warning beacons blazed from England's hilltops and church towers. They met the Armada on Sunday 31 July and Howard issued a formal challenge. The smaller, faster English ships soon had the wind behind them, but dared not sail into the jaws of the mighty Armada's crescent formation.

That night, Drake's *Revenge* drew first blood. Extinguishing the lantern with which he guided the fleet, Drake pursued the damaged Spanish galleon *Rosario*. Upon learning that his attacker was the infamous 'El Draque', her captain, Don Pedro de Valdes, immediately surrendered! Drake treated him with customary hospitality, and learnt from him much of the Armada's plans.

The battling fleets drifted along the English Channel. The Spaniards became more and more infuriated by the nimble English ships' refusal to grapple at close quarters. Finally, on 6 August, the Armada's ships were pinned against the shore of Calais. It was at this point that Sir Francis Drake plotted the destruction of the Spanish forces.

Lord Admiral Howard of Effingham fights with his men against the Spanish might of the Armada.

Devil ships

Out of the darkness, eight shadowy ships drifted silently towards the Armada, their prows dancing with the growing flicker of orange flames. 'Devil ships!' whispered terrified Spanish sailors.

The English had set ablaze eight ships, including Drake's *Thomas* packed with **pitch**, dry timber and tar. At midnight, 7 August, strong winds and tide carried the fire ships into the Armada's heart. As their loaded cannons roared in the heat, the Spanish captains panicked. Fearing explosion they cut their ships' anchor cables and fled.

Daybreak revealed that the great galleass *San Lorenzo* was aground, and only four galleons clustered about their flagship *San Martin*. The rest of the Armada was scattered in disarray to the north-east, drifting without anchors over the grey seas.

A storm separating the battling fleets seemed certain to dash the Spanish ships against the Flemish coast. However, a miraculous change of wind plucked them off the sandbanks and into the North Sea. Pursued by Drake to the Firth of Forth, the Armada was blown around the Scottish coast. Several Spanish ships, their hulls pierced by English shot, foundered and sank. Many were shattered on the jagged west coast of Ireland. Only about half of them ever saw their country again.

When King Philip II learnt of England's victory, it was the Protestant pirate he blamed for the Armada's defeat.

A Spanish wreck in the Irish Sea.

Right *As English 'devil ships' attacked the Armada, the Spanish realized that defeat was inevitable.*

The beating of the drum

Sir Francis Drake was elected Member of Parliament for Plymouth in February 1593, but stayed away from the sea for only two years. On 29 August 1595, he sailed again, for Puerto Rico, where a damaged galleon carrying two and a half million **ducats** was stranded. His reputation as a fearless pirate caused the Spanish to flee their ports. Captaining the *Defiance*, Drake shared command with his old partner Sir John Hawkins.

After failing to conquer Puerto Rico, Drake promised his officers, 'I will bring you to twenty places more wealthy and easier to be gotten.' Drake plundered Rio de la Hacha, Santa Maria and Nombre de Dios. He found little treasure though and lost many of his men in an assault on Panama.

Then **dysentery** ravaged the

On 28 January 1596, Sir Francis Drake died of a fever. His funeral was that of a true sea hero.

fleet, and Drake became ill. Sailing off Portobelo, he raved feverishly in his sleep before donning his armour to meet death as a warrior. He died before sunrise on 28 January 1596. As Drake's coffin was lowered into the sea off Nombre de Dios, the scene of his earliest successes more than twenty years before, Spain celebrated the passing of 'El Draque'.

Drake is remembered as the greatest sea adventurer of the Elizabethan age. However, he was a ruthless, ambitious man who gained wealth by stealing treasures and land from others and who took part in the barbaric but profitable slave trading of the time. According to legend, whenever England faces danger, the beat of his old drum summons Sir Francis Drake once more to her defence.

Sir Francis Drake is remembered for his adventurous voyages.

Important dates

1493   Pope Alexander VI divides discoveries of New World between Portugal and Spain.

1541   Francis Drake born in Tavistock, Devon.

1549   Prayer Book Rebellion forces Drake's family to flee to Kent.

1558   Elizabeth I becomes Queen of England.

1562   John Hawkins' first voyage to the Spanish Main.

1566   Drake makes his first Atlantic crossing.

1568   Drake and Hawkins betrayed by Spanish at San Juan de Ulua.

1569   Drake marries Mary Newman.

1572   Drake captures Nombre de Dios.

1573   Drake sights the Pacific Ocean.

1577   Drake sails around the world in
−80   the *Golden Hind*.

1581   Drake receives knighthood.

1587   Drake 'singes the King of Spain's beard' at Cadiz.

1588   Battle of the Spanish Armada.

1589   Drake's expedition to Portugal.

1595   Drake sails on his last Caribbean voyage.

1596   Drake dies at sea.

Books to read

The Age of Drake by James A. Williamson (A & C Black, 1965)
Sir Francis Drake by Edyth Harper (Ladybird, 1977)
Battle of the Spanish Armada by Roger Hart (Wayland, 1973)

Books for older readers

Francis Drake by Neville Williams (Weidenfeld and Nicholson, 1973)
Sir Francis Drake by George Thomson (Futura, 1972)

Glossary

Apprentice   A young person who is taught a trade through working with an experienced, skilled worker.

Caravel   A small, two- or three-masted sailing ship used during the fifteenth and sixteenth centuries.

Corsair   A pirate.

Doldrums   An area in the sea near the Equator where there is very little wind.

Ducats   Gold coins.

Dysentery   A disease of the intestines causing cramp-like pains and diarrhoea.

Galleasses   Three-masted warships used in the Mediterranean from the fifteenth to the eighteenth centuries.

Gibbet   A wooden framework on which executed criminals were hanged.

Heresy   A belief, especially about religion, which goes against the things that people generally believe.

Hispaniola   The second largest island in the West Indies.

Mariner   A person who travels on the seas; a sailor.

Mercenaries   Soldiers who are paid for fighting in foreign armies.

Mizzen-mast   The rear mast of a ship that has two or three masts.

Mutineers   Members of a ship's crew who rebel against their captain.

Mutiny   Rebellion by the crew of a ship against their captain.

New World   The American continent.

Pennants   Long flags, usually tapering or triangular with one or more tails, flown from ships.

Pike   A weapon used by foot soldiers consisting of a long stick with a metal spearhead.

Pioneering voyage   The first voyage ever made by an explorer to an unknown place.

Pitch   A thick black substance obtained by boiling down tar or turpentine, used in shipbuilding.

Privateer   A member of the crew of a ship sailing in the service of its government.

Scuttle   To sink a ship on purpose by making holes in the bottom.

Shipwrights   People who build ships.

Index

Alexander VI, Pope 5, 6, 9
Atlantic Ocean 10, 17
Azores 23

Cape of Good Hope 19
Cape St Vincent 23
Cape Verde Islands 14
Caribbean 9, 10, 22
    Nombre de Dios 10, 11, 13, 28, 29
Cimaroons 10, 11, 13

Doughty, Thomas 13, 14
Drake, Sir Francis
    birth 6; religion 6–7;
    apprenticeship 7;
    first Atlantic
    crossing 9; first
    marriage 10; attacks
    on Spanish 9, 11, 13,
    16, 17, 22–3, 24–6;
    serves under the Earl
    of Essex 13;
    'privateer' to Queen
    Elizabeth I 13;
    beheads Thomas
    Doughty 14; sails
    Magellan's Strait 14;
    sails around the
    world 19, 20;
    knighted 20–21;
    elected Mayor of
    Plymouth 21; second
    marriage 21; victory
    of the Armada 26;
    elected Member of
    Parliament 28; death
    28–9.
Drake, Edmund 6, 7

Edward VI, King 6
Egypt 14
Elizabeth I, Queen 4, 5, 13, 17, 20, 21, 24
England 4, 9, 13, 15, 18, 21, 22, 26, 29
English Channel 4, 7, 24

Fever 13, 22, 29
Fleming, Captain Thomas 5

Golden Hind 14, 15, 16, 17, 18, 19, 20, 21
Guatemala 17

Hatton, Sir Christopher 15
Hawkins, Sir John 9, 28
Howard, Lord Admiral 5, 24

Indian Ocean 19
Indonesia 18
Ireland 13, 26

Magellan, Ferdinand 14, 15
Magellan's Strait 15
Martin, Don 9
Mendoza, Spanish ambassador 20, 21
Mexico 9
Mocha Islands 16

New World 9
Newman, Mary 10
North America 16, 17
North Sea 26

Pacific Ocean 10, 11, 13, 15, 18

Panama Isthmus 10, 11, 13, 16, 28
Peru 16
Philip II, King 4, 13, 20, 22, 23, 26
Pirates 5, 9, 10, 13, 26, 28
Plymouth 5, 9, 13, 14, 19, 22, 23, 24, 28
Portugal 9, 14
Port St Julian 14
Protestantism 4, 6, 7, 26

Rebellion 13, 14, 18
Rio de la Hacha 9, 28
Roman Catholicism 4, 6

San Juan de Ulua 9, 10
Sierra Leone 19
South America 9, 14, 16
Spain 4, 9, 13, 21, 22, 24, 26, 29
Spanish Armada 4, 5, 10, 13, 22, 23, 24, 26
Spice Islands 18
Sydenham, Elizabeth 21

Testu, Guillaume Le 13
Treasure 11, 13, 16, 20, 21, 23, 24, 28, 29

de Valdes, Don Pedro 24
Voyages 7, 9, 10, 13, 14, 19, 20, 22

Walter, Earl of Essex 13
West Indies 9

de Zarate, Don Francisco 17